The Navajo

Geraldine Woods

Watts LIBRARY

Franklin Watts
A Division of Scholastic Inc.
New York • Toronto • London • Auckland • Sydney
Mexico City • New Delhi • Hong Kong
Danbury, Connecticut

Note to readers: Definitions for words in **bold** can be found in the Glossary at the back of this book.

Photographs ©: AP/Wide World Photos: 37 left, 37 right (Cumberland County Historical Society), 46; Arthur Shilstone: 33, 34; Corbis-Bettmann: 7 (Tom Bean), 20 (Robert Holmes), 18 (Buddy Mays), 38 (Charles E. Rotkin); North Wind Picture Archives: 28, 31; Photo Researchers, NY: 41 (Emil Muench), 48 (Portefield/Chickering); Place Stock Photo: 12, 17; Smithsonian Institution, Washington, DC: 35; Stone: 24, 25 (Paul Chesley), 10 (Sylvain Grandadam), 6 (Paul Wakefield); Sun Valley Video & Photography: 44 (Marilyn "Angel" Wynn), 26; Viesti Collection, Inc.: 3 top, 9; Woodfin Camp & Associates: 3 bottom, 43, 49 (Dan Budnik), 47 (Michal Heron), 15 (Suzi Moore), 42 (National Archives), 23 (Adam Woolfitt).

Map by XNR Productions Inc.

Cover illustration by Gary Overacre, interpreted from a photograph from Corbis-Bettmann.

Library of Congress Cataloging-in-Publication Data

Woods, Geraldine.
    The Navajo / by Geraldine Woods
        p. cm—(Watts library)
    Includes bibliographical references and index.
    ISBN 0-531-13950-6 (lib. bdg.)   0-531-16227-3 (pbk.)
    1. Navajo Indians—Juvenile literature. [1. Navajo Indians. 2. Indians of North America—Southwest, New.] I. Title. II. Series.
E99.N3 W748 2002
979.1'004972—dc21

2001017593

Contents

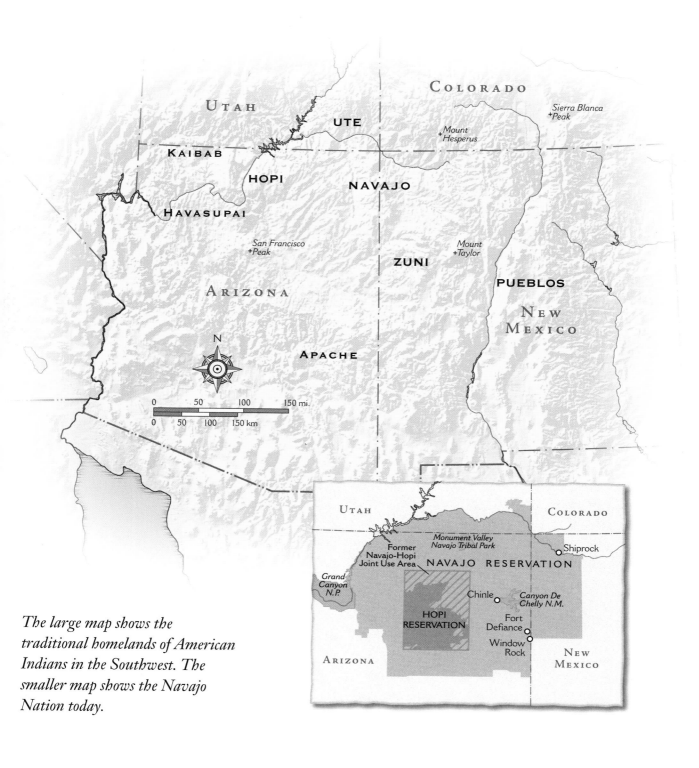

The large map shows the traditional homelands of American Indians in the Southwest. The smaller map shows the Navajo Nation today.

Chapter One

Ancient Land, Ancient People

A traditional song of the Navajo celebrates their beloved homeland:

"This is your home, my grandchild!"
He says to me as he sits down beside me;
"My grandchild!
I have returned with you to your home!"

The land of the Navajo is in the southwestern United States. It occupies parts of three states—Arizona, New Mexico, and Utah. The Navajo Nation lies between the four sacred mountains:

Monument Valley has been used as a setting for many movies.

Sierra Blanca Peak in the east, Mount Taylor in the south, San Francisco Peak in the west, and Mount Hesperus in the north. It is a place of great beauty. Tall mountains covered in pine trees, huge rocks, and deep canyons create awesome landscapes. There are many **mesas**—flat-topped hills—as well as valleys and rolling plains.

Many places in the Navajo Nation look familiar, even to people who have never been there. That's because film directors often use its dramatic landscape in their works. For example, Monument Valley, with its startling red rock towers and cliffs, has been in countless movies and commercials.

Window Rock

The capital of the Navajo Nation is Window Rock—named for a huge rock formation with a hole in the center.

Most of the Navajo Nation is desert or very dry land. Only the mountains have a good amount of rainfall. Evergreen trees grow in the mountains. Plants that need little water, such as sagebrush, pinyon, and some grasses, grow on the plains and in the valleys. Since much of the Navajo Nation is high above sea level, summer temperatures may be mild, but very hot days are possible in summer, especially in the valleys. Winters are fairly mild as well, except in the mountains, where temperatures often drop below freezing. Bears, coyotes, mountain lions, and deer live in the Navajo Nation, as well as rabbits, prairie dogs, and other small animals. Lizards and snakes are also found there.

Canyon de Chelly

Canyon de Chelly, a national monument, contains ruins dating from A.D. 360 as well as modern Navajo homes and farms.

7

The Mysterious Beginning

Where did the Navajo come from? The Navajo believe that human beings traveled through several other worlds before they reached the Earth where we live today. The Navajo, who call themselves *Dine*, meaning "the People," believe that they were created from Mother Earth and Father Sky. The *Dine* are a part of the land, a part of their Mother's beauty.

According to one theory, the ancient ancestors of today's Navajo may have lived in Asia, in the region of Mongolia. During the last Ice Age thousands of years ago, some of these people may have crossed into North America by walking across a narrow strip of land between the two continents. (That land bridge, if it did exist, is now underwater.) The tribe gradually moved south from Canada into what is now the United States. Navajo is a member of the Athapascan family of languages. There are tribes in Canada that speak Athapascan languages, as do the Apache of the Southwest. This language family may tell us where the Navajo once lived.

Another theory is that the Navajo's ancestors once lived south or west of their present homeland, perhaps in what is now California. Then they moved east and north. Wherever they came from, a good number of Navajo were in the Southwest by the 1300s. Scientists have also found scattered remains of Navajo settlements dating from about a thousand years ago, so some Navajo arrived even earlier.

The Navajo were not the first people to live in the Southwest, however. A more ancient people had settled there

Navajo, Navaho, or Dine?

In their own language, the Navajo are *Dine*. Spanish explorers called the tribe *Navajo*. Sometimes the word is spelled "Navaho."

There are many theories about how the Navajo came to live in the Southwest.

Weaving

According to legend, the Navajo learned how to weave from Spider Woman. Most weavers are women, working on handlooms outside in the dry desert air. The patterns vary, but shades of red, white, and gray are popular.

Navajo weavers always weave a line from the center of the pattern to the edge. The legend says that without this line, Spider Woman will spin her webs in the mind of the weaver and drive the weaver mad.

centuries before. The Navajo called these people the *Anasazi*, meaning "our enemies." The Anasazi moved away from Navajo territory in the 1300s, probably because of a shortage of water. Their descendants, the Pueblo Indians, became the Navajo's neighbors. The Pueblos taught the *Dine* weaving and many farming skills. The Navajo grew corn, beans, and melons and hunted animals.

The Anasazi

The Anasazi lived in cliff dwellings that looked like apartment houses.

The Spanish Arrive

In the 1500s, Spanish explorers and settlers reached Navajo territory. Their soldiers rode horses, and the settlers raised long-haired sheep and goats, which they had brought with them from Europe. The Navajo soon captured some animals and established herds of their own. The wool from the sheep was excellent for weaving, and Navajo blankets and rugs became prized trade goods. By the late 1600s, the Navajo's most important occupation was raising sheep, cattle, and goats.

Throughout the centuries, the *Dine* learned many new customs from their Indian and Mexican neighbors. Today, their lifestyle has changed, but many ancient Navajo traditions survive.

This hogan serves as a visitor center at Canyon de Chelly in Arizona.

Chapter Two

A Traditional Life

Anyone who travels through the Navajo Nation today will see many modern houses and trailers. Visitors will also notice a much more ancient type of dwelling—the **hogan**. The hogan, a traditional Navajo house, is eight-sided or round. The hogan is warm in winter and cool in summer. Old-style hogans were made of tree branches and soil. Where trees were scarce, hogans were built of stone. The floor is made of hard-packed dirt.

The door of a hogan always faces east to catch the rising sun. Newer hogans have windows and may be constructed of modern building materials. Inside, the hogan is one large room about 20 feet (6 meters) across. Benches and storage spaces line the walls, and a stove or fireplace sits in the center of the room. Traditionally, the family sleeps on bedrolls. In mild weather, activities such as weaving and cooking may take place outdoors.

Many families have more than one hogan—perhaps keeping one for religious ceremonies and one to live in. Special small hogans are made for sweat baths. (In a sweat bath, steam makes the body sweat and thus cleanse itself.) Some families build summer hogans and winter hogans, each near the spot where their sheep spend the season.

The Clan System

Traditionally, the most important person in a Navajo family is the mother. When two people marry, the husband joins his wife's family. The women have the right to the land set aside for them by their families. They own the house, the sheep, and the goats. The women also have the right to keep any money they earn from weaving. The men own the horses, the wages from their jobs, and any items or money they brought into the marriage.

Both men and women take care of the children. Elderly family members often help out as well. Navajo babies are sometimes strapped into padded wooden packs called

No Mother-in-Law Trouble!

Navajo men and their mothers-in-law are not allowed to talk to—or even to look at—each other. This custom probably reduces the number of family arguments!

cradleboards. Navajo parents believe that cradleboards give their babies straight backs and shoulders. Traditionally, the father makes the cradleboard for his child, singing, "I make a baby-board for you, my child. May you grow to a great old age." Children play an important role in a Navajo family. Even when they are very young, Navajo children care for some of the family's sheep or help with grown-up chores.

The very young and the very old are given much love and care in a traditional Navajo family. *Hosteen*, a Navajo word meaning "old man," is a title of great respect. Elderly women may be addressed as "Grandmother," even if they are not related to the speaker.

Each family belongs to a larger group called a **clan**. When Navajo people introduce themselves, they first say which clan they are "born to" (the mother's clan) and "born for" (the father's clan). If anything happens to the parents, the mother's clan decides who will care for the children. Marriage within clans is not permitted, though today this rule is not always followed.

A Navajo mother watches over her baby sleeping on a cradleboard.

The Bitter Water, the Mud, the Folded Arms People, and the Little Deer are some of the sixty or so Navajo clans. Clan members are expected to help one another in every way possible. The clan structure keeps order in the tribe. If one clan member misbehaves, everyone is shamed. As a result, in order to uphold the honor of the clan, individuals feel pressure to behave properly. One of the worst insults is to say that a Navajo "acts as if he or she has no relatives."

Clothing of the Navajo

Long ago, Navajo women wore simple dresses made of two blankets sewn together, with holes for the neck and arms. In the 1800s, long full skirts and bright velveteen blouses became popular styles for women. Navajo men wore long shirts, first sleeveless and later with sleeves attached. Both men and women wore moccasins with thick white-leather soles and high deerskin tops.

Navajo men also wore leggings. Sometimes the leggings were made of leather, but more often they were knitted. A

Navajo man usually knitted his own leggings. Often the knitter even made his own knitting needles! Thin pieces of metal, perhaps spokes from an old umbrella, were fashioned into needles. So were twigs from a bush or a tree. The yarn was blue, black, or white in color.

Navajo men and women now wear the same styles of clothing as any other Americans. But there is often a special Navajo touch. The *Dine* are excellent silversmiths, having learned the craft from Mexican silversmiths in the 1800s. So most Navajo families own some silver and **turquoise** jewelry. Men and women often wear silver belts. A popular silver pattern is the **squash blossom**, shaped like the flowers of the squash plant.

What's for Dinner?

In a land with so many sheep, it is not surprising that stew made of **mutton** (a meat from sheep) is a popular dish. The stew might be eaten with

The necklace that this woman wears is an example of the jewelry with the squash blossom pattern.

This photograph shows a Navajo woman making fry bread on a skillet outside.

fry bread, wheat dough that is fried in hot oil. When the Navajo were first introduced to wheat in the 1800s, they did not know how to cook it, and many people became ill. Now fry bread is a Navajo specialty. Kneel Down Bread, which is shaped like a kneeling person, is another Navajo favorite. Kneel Down Bread is made of corn.

The Navajo eat the same kinds of food you might find anywhere, including fast food. One special "Navajo fast food" is pinyon nuts, the seeds of a type of pine tree. They may be eaten raw or roasted.

Some Navajo will not eat seafood. According to legend, as the *Dine* passed from one world into another, some stayed behind and lived in the water. To eat seafood, therefore, is to risk eating a relative.

Trading Posts

In the late 1800s, trading posts were the only stores in Navajo territory. There the Navajo could exchange weaving, jewelry, and other products for food and merchandise.

*In the creation
story of the Navajo,
the First World was
an island.*

Chapter Three

The Navajo Way

The Navajo, like people everywhere, tell stories about their own creation. According to the Navajo story, in the beginning all was darkness. The First World was an island. In the water surrounding it lived the Water Monster. The Insect People lived in the First World—red ants, dragonflies, beetles, and others. The People quarreled, and their chiefs said they must go elsewhere. The People squeezed through a slit in the sky into the Second World.

The Second World was the world of Bird People. Again the People quarreled, and soon, guided by the Wind, they flew to a hole in the sky. There they found the Third World, the land of the Grasshopper People. Only one river flowed through the bare land. Soon the People left the Third World and found the Fourth, where the mountains were covered with snow. There the People met the Pueblo Indians, who guided the People to a river with red water. The Pueblos gave the People corn and pumpkins and taught them how to **irrigate** their crops.

In the Fourth World, the People began to look like human beings for the first time. Deerskins, corn, and eagle feathers were placed on the ground. The winds gave them life, creating First Man and First Woman. The earth and the sky met, and Coyote and Badger were born. One day, Coyote—a troublemaker—stole two babies from the Water Monster. The Water Monster sent a flood to punish the People, but the people escaped through a hollow reed into the Fifth World. They sent the babies back to the Water Monster, and the waters drained away.

Changing Woman and the Hero Twins

One day First Man found a baby, who grew into Changing Woman. Changing Woman represents the Earth and life. Changing Woman and her sister, White Shell Woman, each gave birth to a son. (In some versions of this story, White Shell

How Many Worlds?

Many versions of the Navajo creation story exist today. In some, the People now live in the Fourth World.

22

Monster Blood

The dried lava flows in the Navajo Nation are said to be the blood of the monsters killed by the Hero Twins.

Woman gives birth to both boys.) The boys went on a magical journey to find their father—the Sun. They had to pass many tests before he would accept them. Once the Sun was sure that the boys were indeed his sons, he gave them magic weapons. The Hero Twins returned to earth to kill the monsters that were attacking the People.

These stories, with many variations, are part of the religion of the *Dine*. The Navajo's traditional religion is sometimes called **the Way**—a code of behavior that governs every part of

Navajo life. This religion is not something that is celebrated only once a week in a church or temple. It is a series of daily actions.

Certain values are part of the Navajo Way. The land and the animals should be respected because they were given to human beings by the **Holy People**, the Navajo gods. The *Dine* should help one another, not try to obtain personal wealth or fame. If the People do not respect tradition, misfortune will come to the tribe.

Ceremonies

Navajo ceremonies are called **ways**. One of the most important is the **Nightway**, a nine-day healing ceremony. During the Nightway, friends and relatives of a sick person gather. A special hogan is built, and a **singer**, a religious leader, sings special songs. The singer also uses crushed rock of many colors to create sacred pictures. These pictures are called **sand paintings**, or dry paintings. After the ceremony is over, the pictures are swept up and the sand is taken away.

*Inside a hogan, Navajo create
a traditional sand painting.*

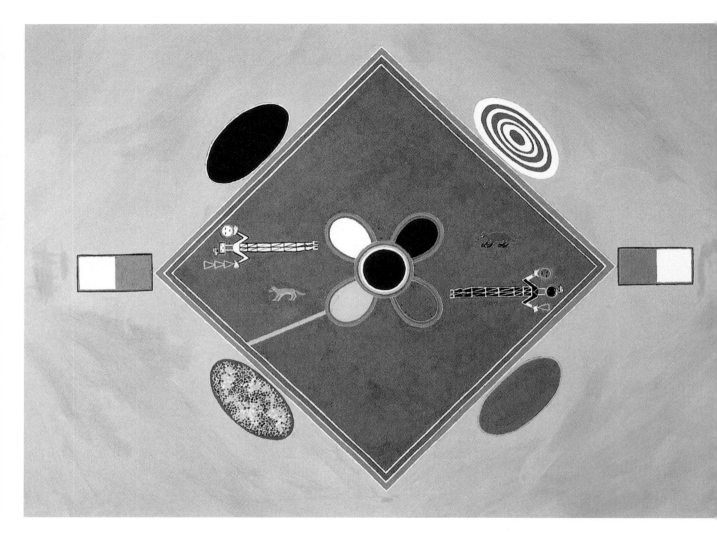

This sand painting is from a blessingway ceremony.

An **Enemyway** is a three-day event for a Navajo returning from non-Navajo society. The ceremony cleanses the Navajo of foreign influences. Another ceremony marks the coming of age of Navajo girls. A special corn cake is baked, and everyone eats a little of it. At a Navajo wedding, the bride and the groom are each given the **pollen**, or seed, of corn. Still other ceremonies bless new hogans or celebrate the birth of babies.

All these ceremonies are important to the *Dine*. The ceremonial songs are treasures. One Navajo man once commented, "I have always been a poor man. I do not know a single song."

There are no traditional Navajo funeral ceremonies. The Navajo believe that death takes the best part of each person into another world, a world that the People were in before they arrived on Earth. The ghost stays on Earth, where it can harm the living. The body is buried as quickly as possible, often by a non-Navajo.

All Navajo ceremonies have one purpose: to create harmony between the *Dine* and the natural world. Harmony flows from respect for tradition, respect for the Navajo Way.

Sacred Corn

Corn or corn pollen is sacred and plays an important role in the Navajo Way.

The arrival of the Spanish in the 1500s caused suffering and heartbreak for the Navajo.

Chapter Four

Outsiders Arrive

The Spanish explorers who arrived in the Southwest in the 1500s amazed the *Dine*. One Zuni Indian who saw these strangers described them as wearing "coats of iron." The newcomers carried guns—"short canes" that made "thunder." They were looking for cities made of gold. These imaginary cities, described in many legends, were called "The Seven Cities of Cíbola." Of course, the Spanish never found Cíbola. However, the **conquistadors**, the Spanish conquerors, found something else they wanted—land to colonize and claim for Spain.

The Spanish never succeeded in controlling the Navajo. The *Dine* were too spread out and too fierce. However, the Spanish reign in the Southwest was a time of trouble for the tribe. The Spanish often raided Navajo settlements, killing the men and stealing women and children. The women and children were then taken to Mexico, a Spanish colony, as slaves. When Mexico gained its independence from Spain in 1821, the Southwest became a territory of Mexico called New Mexico. Although the Mexicans and not the Spanish were now in charge, the raids continued.

The *Dine* fought back. They raided New Mexican settlements, also killing adults and capturing children. The New Mexican children, however, did not have to live as slaves as the captured Navajo did. The New Mexican children were adopted into the Navajo tribe and treated as equals.

The United States Takes Over

In 1848, Mexico lost a war with the United States. The treaty gave much of the Southwest—including the Navajo homeland—to the United States. The Navajo thought that the U.S. government would be friendly to them. After all, the Mexicans had been the enemy of both the Navajo and the Americans. But the *Dine* soon learned that little had changed. The descendents of the Spanish settlers continued their raids. So did other Indian tribes, such as the Ute and the Apache.

During this period more and more white settlers were moving into the Southwest from other parts of the United States. They wanted Indian land, and they wanted the government to help them get it. In many parts of the United States, Indians had already been removed from their homelands and sent to **reservations**. Reservations are land areas set aside just for American Indians. Frequently the reservations were on land considered less valuable by whites. And once the Indians were on reservations, their homelands were opened to white settlers.

Most whites of the time did not think twice about taking land away from the American Indians because most white people did not view the Indians as equals. In fact, Indians were

When the settlers moved into the Southwest, they wanted to take over land from the Indians.

often seen simply as obstacles to white "progress." The white governor of the New Mexico Territory was typical. In 1863, he spoke of the fine grazing and minerals of the Navajo land. He urged that the area be taken away from the tribe because the Navajo had too long been "lords of the soil."

The Navajo saw the situation differently, of course. They believed that they had been led to their homeland by their gods—the Holy People. So the Navajo refused to give their land up. They defended their homeland fiercely.

Many times during the mid-1800s the *Dine* and the U.S. representatives met for peace talks. But none of the talks were successful for long. Part of the problem was a lack of communication. Few Americans spoke Navajo, and few Navajo spoke English. Also, whenever the Americans tried to write a treaty, they asked to speak to the chief of the Navajo. But the Navajo had no chief. Small groups of *Dine* might recognize one wise "headman," but all the adults of the group generally made decisions together. Among the Navajo, one small group did not speak for all the people.

The Americans would ask the Navajo to send a "chief" to sign an agreement. An elder, often not understanding anything of the conversation, would make an X on a piece of paper. The Americans then believed that all the *Dine* were committed to the treaty. In fact, most *Dine* knew absolutely nothing about it! Soon the Americans, accusing the Navajo of breaking the treaty, would launch more raids, and the Navajo would retaliate with raids of their own.

The Long Walk

By 1863, the U.S. government had seen enough raids and counter-raids. Also, whites thought there might be valuable minerals on Navajo land. The plan was to move the Navajo to a distant reservation.

That's when Colonel Christopher "Kit" Carson, a famous hunter and scout, was called in. The U.S. Army had given him the task of defeating the Navajo. Carson ordered his soldiers to shoot all Navajo on sight—men, women, and children. Carson also went after the Navajo's food supply. He sent his soldiers throughout Navajo territory, burning crops, killing livestock, and destroying homes.

In February 1864, the Navajo began to give up. In small groups they journeyed to army forts and surrendered. The Long Walk began. Each group of *Dine* walked for almost three weeks to Bosque Redondo, a camp that had been set up for the tribe. Hundreds died along the way.

When the Navajo arrived at the Bosque Redondo camp, it was clear that life there would be harsh.

On orders from Colonel Carson, soldiers destroyed the Navajo's food supply.

The Navajo were forced to walk nearly 300 miles (480 km) to Bosque Redondo. Many suffered and died along the way. Some estimates say that 8,000 Navajo Indians took part in the Long Walk.

The land was bare because most of the trees had been cut down to build Fort Sumner, the army's headquarters. The Navajo had to walk for hours to gather firewood. The water was full of bitter minerals and not fit to drink. The crops failed, and the army gave the tribe only poor-quality food. Many Navajo became ill. The animals and seed they had been promised never arrived. Away from their sacred homeland, the tribe suffered spiritually as well. In the first year alone, two thousand Navajo died.

Return to Navajo Territory

After four years in Bosque Redondo, the people were desperate. A Navajo named Ganado Mucho pleaded with the

Americans. "We want to go back to our own country," he said. "The land here will never be as good . . . we were born to live in our old country . . . we were not born to live here."

In 1868, the *Dine* were finally allowed to return to the land of the four sacred mountains. Many wept with happiness as they caught their first glimpse of Navajo territory. But some wept tears of sorrow. Their homeland had nearly been destroyed. The croplands were overgrown with weeds, and the peach trees, the corn, the melon fields—all were gone. Most of the animals were dead. Even though they had arrived, the *Dine* still faced a long road back.

The 1868 treaty that the Navajo signed created the Navajo Reservation, which included only about 10 percent of the land that the tribe had lost. Land was added to the reservation several times over the years, but it has never returned to its original size.

The treaty also promised that the *Dine* would never again make war on the United States. The U.S. government, in turn, said it would give each Navajo family two sheep and enough food to get through the year, as

Barboncito

Barboncito, a great leader of the *Dine*, convinced the U.S. government to allow the Navajo to return to their territory.

The Largest Reservation

The Navajo Nation, the largest reservation in the United States, has more land than Massachusetts, New Hampshire, and Vermont combined. It covers 16 million acres (6.5 million hectares).

well as seed and supplies for farming. The government also promised to create schools and supply teachers for Navajo children.

The *Dine* kept their promise, but the United States did not. Very few supplies arrived in Navajo territory, and only a few schools were set up. Nevertheless, the Navajo rebuilt their nation.

Kill the Indian, Save the Man

As the *Dine* entered the twentieth century, they faced great pressure from white society. At that time, most whites believed that Indians should give up their traditional ways. As one popular saying put it, "Kill the Indian, save the man." In other words, the whites wanted to destroy the "Indian" in each Navajo—the customs, language, and beliefs of the *Dine*. One of the ways that whites carried out this policy was by controlling the schools.

Whites ran all the schools on the reservation. Many were boarding schools because it was impractical for Navajo children from remote areas to travel to school every day. In boarding schools whites were in charge of a child's whole life.

At school, the Navajo children were punished for speaking their own language. They were mocked for following traditional customs, and some were forced to accept a new religion. Many children, exposed for the first time to new diseases, sickened and died. Some ran away, and most were very homesick. One Navajo student said that when she went to boarding

school, "My heart ached too for my parents, my home, my lambs, and my rock toys left behind."

Successful students often returned to their families feeling torn between two worlds. After many years in a white school, where did they fit? The white world often looked down upon them simply for being Indians, but the Indian world no longer seemed like home. To their own parents, they had become strangers. The boarding schools were one of the white world's attempts to destroy Navajo culture. That attempt, like all the others, did not succeed.

The photograph on the left shows a Navajo named Tom Torlino in 1887 when he arrived at the Carlisle Indian School in Pennsylvania. The photograph on the right shows what Tom looked like in 1890 after completing school.

The promise of "black gold," or oil, brought outsiders to the lands of the Navajo in the 1900s.

Chapter Five

A Nation Is Formed

With its sweeping desert views and towering mountains, the land of the Navajo is filled with beauty. Plus, it was a gift to the *Dine* from the Holy People. It was always obvious to the Navajo that their land was valuable, but the Navajo territory for a time seemed less desirable to others. Farming and grazing were not easy with so little water. Then in 1922 whites discovered that the land of the Navajo contained something they wanted—oil.

As white companies prepared contracts for Navajo oil, a problem arose. Who would sign the contracts? The *Dine* still had a local system of government. The most respected elder of each small group of Navajo made the decisions, usually by reaching an agreement with all the adults in the group. But no one person spoke for all of the people.

The *Dine* formed a tribal council in 1923 with Chee Dodge as its head. For the first time the Navajo had a central government. However, its powers were limited. The Bureau of Indian Affairs (BIA) continued to control many aspects of Navajo life. The tribal council quickly arranged for the sale or rent of mineral rights.

Too Many Animals?

The Navajo worked long and hard to rebuild their animal herds after they returned from Bosque Redondo. They were successful—in fact, they were too successful. By 1900, there were too many animals grazing in Navajo territory, and the land was becoming bare. In 1926 the council asked the *Dine* to limit the number of animals. But the program was voluntary, and few people went along with it.

A few years later, BIA agents forced the Navajo to reduce their herds. The plan was to kill a certain number of sheep and goats and sell the meat. But there was not enough money to ship the meat to market. So the animals were simply shot and left to rot on the ground. To the *Dine*, such waste was an offense against nature. One Navajo commented sadly that the

The Bureau of Indian Affairs' decision to reduce the number of sheep and goats on the reservation caused great hardship for the Navajo.

government official "stomped his big foot on our sheep, goats, and horses—and crushed them before our eyes."

Because of the killing, many Navajo became very poor. They had lived off their herds, and now most of the animals were dead. One Navajo woman said, "All around Indians are hungry and traders don't give credit any more . . . Indian agency bring food in cans. If not Indian must beg from white man who visits." However, overall the program did work. The land recovered, and eventually the animals in the Navajo herds were healthier. They produced more wool and meat than they had before.

The Navajo Code Talkers

During World War II (1939–1945) when the United States was at war with Japan, the Navajo Nation sent 3,600 men and

World War II Brings Change

In 1941, when the United States became involved in World War II, many Navajo worked off the reservation for the first time.

Two Navajo code talkers relay orders on a field radio.

12 women to military service. Four hundred of those Navajo helped their country in a very special way. Time and again, the Japanese broke the American military codes. Navajo Marines created a code in their own language, which was known to few non-Navajo.

The code talkers chose one word in Navajo for each letter. They also used Navajo words for military terms. An "owl," for example, was an observation plane. A "turtle" was a tank. An "egg" (bomb) was dropped by a "buzzard" (bomber). Navajo clan names were used for military units.

Soon a whole network of Navajo **code talkers** was set up. Though the Japanese broke the codes used by the U.S. Army, Navy, and Air Force, they never broke the Marines' Navajo code. The code talkers' work remained secret until 1968. In recent years the code talkers have received many honors from the U.S. government.

Uranium Is Discovered

World War II ended with an American victory in 1945 after two atomic bombs were dropped on Japan. Suddenly the materials needed to make the bombs became extremely valuable. In 1951 one of the key ingredients—**uranium**—was discovered in the Navajo Nation. A number of mines quickly opened, employing many Navajo.

However, uranium is a dangerous material that gives off **radiation**. In large quantities its invisible rays can kill. In smaller amounts, radiation may cause cancer and other deadly diseases. So uranium must be mined very carefully to protect the workers and the environment.

The mining companies were not careful. In fact, they did not even tell the Navajo people about the dangers. As a result, workers returned to their homes with uranium dust on their clothes. Piles of radioactive waste sat near people and animals, and some of the waste fell into the water supply. Many Navajo sickened and died. Only years later did the tribe find out what had happened. In 1990, Congress passed a law giving money to the Navajo people who had been hurt by uranium mining.

NASA in the Navajo Nation

NASA practiced moon landings in the Navajo Nation because its surface is similar to that of the moon.

This photograph shows the remains of a uranium mine, which is now closed.

Raising animals remains an important part of Navajo life.

Chapter Six

The Navajo Today

Today, a visitor to the lands of the Navajo will see a mixture of the modern and the traditional. Some Navajo live in houses while others live in hogans. Many Navajo follow in their ancestors' footsteps by farming the land, raising sheep, and practicing traditional crafts, such as weaving and pottery. Others work as mining engineers, health care professionals, and lawyers. The twenty-first century has arrived in the Navajo Nation, but the *Dine* have kept much of the past too.

Kelsey Begaye, president of the Navajo Nation, works in his office in Window Rock, Arizona.

The Navajo Nation

The Navajo Reservation set up by the treaty of 1868 is now the Navajo Nation, an indication of the increased power and responsibility that the tribal government has assumed in recent years. The *Dine* have a president, a congress, and a court system. About a hundred **chapters**, divisions of local government, send representatives to the capital at Window Rock.

Instead of outsiders, Navajo now run many of the schools, and even those schools staffed by non-Indians have changed. No longer do teachers attempt to "kill the Indian." Respect

for tradition, classes in Navajo as well as in English, and a celebration of Indian culture are the rule.

Children attending a Navajo boarding school take a break from their classes.

But many problems remain. Children must still travel long distances to day schools or leave their families to live in boarding schools. Too many schools lack basic necessities—books, computers, and other equipment. The dropout rate is high.

Dine College

Would you like to learn Navajo? Perhaps you should enroll in *Dine* College. Established in 1968, it was the first college established by American Indians in the United States. The college offers degrees in Navajo culture, Navajo history and Indian Studies, and Navajo language. It also offers degrees in computer science, business, psychology, environmental science, and many other subjects.

Many Navajo homes lack what many others take for granted—electricity and running water.

The unemployment rate is also high—more than 50 percent in recent years. Those who do not wish to work on the land often have to leave the Navajo Nation and find a job elsewhere. In 2000, about 25 percent of the tribe were "city Navajo," and that number is expected to double over the next ten years.

The tribe must meet other challenges too. Only 60 percent of the homes in the Navajo Nation have electricity, and only 23 percent have telephones. Many houses have neither running water nor plumbing.

A Growing Nation

In 2000, the tribe's population numbered about 250,000.

Whose Land?
The Navajo's or the Hopi's?

In 1882, the U.S. government created a Hopi reservation inside the Navajo reservation. The Hopi are one of the Pueblo peoples who have been the Navajo's neighbors for centuries. As the Navajo population increased, some *Dine* began to use lands that the Hopi felt belonged to them. In 1958, the Hopi sued the Navajo, claiming that the *Dine* were trespassing on Hopi land. The court then created an area that both tribes could share—the "joint use area."

It was hard for the two tribes to agree on how to use that land, however. So in 1974, Congress divided the land into two sections. The Navajo who were living on Hopi land were

Federal officials, tribal lawyers, and Navajo from the Big Mountain area meet to discuss the conflict with the Hopi over land.

supposed to move away, as were the Hopi who were living in the Navajo section. Many deadlines for moving have come and gone, and the matter is still not settled. Even now, some Navajo refuse to leave their homes, and the tribes continue to argue about this territory.

Living in Two Worlds

Can the Navajo Way guide the *Dine* in the modern world? Lori Arviso Alvord thinks so. As a Navajo surgeon, she practices up-to-date, scientific medicine, but she also respects the *Dine* healing ceremonies. In fact, when she was pregnant, she went to a singer who conducted a blessing ceremony for her baby.

Fred Begay is another Navajo who has made a bridge between two worlds. His parents were Navajo healers, while he holds a doctorate in nuclear physics and has worked for the space program. Begay often speaks to students about the elements of science found in the Navajo Way. For example, the Navajo traditionally count their sheep in groups of eight. Begay points out that eight is also the most important number in the arithmetic of computer science.

Begay and Arviso Alvord are part of the future of the *Dine*, a future that includes the best Navajo traditions. Like them, the *Dine* will combine the Navajo Way with the best of the twenty-first century.

Navajo Detectives

Tony Hillerman has written many mystery novels set in the Navajo Nation. His detectives are two Navajo police officers.

Timeline

1000	Scattered settlements of Navajo live in the Southwest.
1400	A large number of Navajo live in the Southwest.
1540	Spanish explorers arrive in Navajo territory, bringing sheep, goats, and horses.
1583	Antonio de Espejo, a Spanish explorer, writes of his visit to a Hopi village and Navajo in the area south of Mount Taylor.
1598	The first missionary assignments to the Navajo are made by Spanish priests.
1600	Spanish colonists begin to raid Navajo settlements, stealing women and children as slaves. Navajo, with horses obtained from the Spanish, raid Spanish settlements.
1640	The Navajo and the Pueblo unite to fight the Spanish.
1680	The Navajo learn the Pueblo weaving technique and begin to create their own style.
1700	Livestock raising becomes important in the Navajo economy.
1720–70	Brief period of peace between the Navajo and the Spanish.
1770	War raids between the Spanish and the Navajo begin again.
1805	Spanish soldiers attack the Navajo in Canyon de Chelly. Many Navajo are killed.
1821	Mexico wins its independence from Spain. Navajo country is part of a territory called New Mexico ruled by Mexico.
1824	The Bureau of Indian Affairs is established.

continued next page

Timeline *continued*

1846–48	Mexico and the United States fight the Mexican-American War. The United States wins.
1851	U.S. Army builds Fort Defiance in Navajo Territory.
1860	A thousand Navajo attack Fort Defiance, almost winning until they are driven back by superior guns.
1863	Colonel Kit Carson begins a bloody campaign against the Navajo.
1864	The Long Walk to Bosque Redondo removes almost all the Navajo from their homeland.
1864–68	The Navajo reach the Bosque Redondo camp. Many die from the bad conditions there.
1868	A treaty between the U.S. government and the Navajo allows the tribe to return to their homeland.
1882	President Chester A. Arthur creates the Hopi Reservation in Northern Arizona.
1893	Nineteen Navajo leaders attend the Columbian Exhibition—a world's fair—in Chicago.
1922	Oil is discovered on Navajo land. The Bureau of Indian Affairs creates a Navajo Business Council to negotiate oil leases.
1923	The Business Council becomes the basis for a central Navajo government.
1924	U.S. government passes the Indian Citizenship Act, making Indians citizens of the United States. Navajo are now allowed to vote in national elections but not in state or local elections.
1928	Navajo women receive the right to vote in tribal elections.

1930	U.S. government investigation finds that Navajo children are being kidnapped and taken to boarding schools against the wishes of their families.
1932–36	More than 250,000 sheep and goats are killed by agents of the Bureau of Indian Affairs to prevent overgrazing.
1934	Congress passes the Indian Reorganization Act, which gives Indian tribal governments rights and responsibilities in relation to the federal government. The Navajo reject the bill.
1938	The Indian Lands Mining Act is passed, giving the federal government some decision-making power over mineral rights on Indian lands.
1941	When the United States enters World War II, all American Indian men are required to register for the draft.
1942–45	Navajo Code Talkers send secret messages in the Pacific, helping to defeat the Japanese.
1947	U.S. court rules that the Hopi and Navajo tribes should share equally in mineral rights for land held by both tribes.
1948	Arizona and New Mexico allow the Navajo to vote in state and local elections.
1950	Congress passes the Navajo-Hopi Rehabilitation Act. Money is set aside to build roads, schools, and irrigation projects on the reservations.
1951	Uranium is discovered on Navajo land.
1957	Utah allows the Navajo to vote in state and local elections.
1958	A special court is set up to settle the question of ownership of land where both Navajo and Hopi live.
1960s	Navajo begin to have more control over their schools. Education in both English and Navajo is introduced.

continued next page

Timeline *continued*

1962	The court creates a Navajo-Hopi Joint Use Area. Both tribes have equal ownership.
1969	Navajo Community College, now called *Dine* College, is established.
1974	Congress passes the Navajo Relocation Act, requiring about 12,000 Navajo to leave land in the Joint Use Area.
1979	The largest nuclear accident in the United States takes place on Navajo land. More than 1,000 tons of uranium waste gushes through a broken dam.
1982	President Ronald Reagan declares National Navajo Code Talkers Day.
1986	The final deadline for the Navajo to leave the Hopi-Navajo Joint Use lands. Despite the deadline, some Navajo remain.
1990	Congress passes a law giving money to Navajo people harmed by uranium mining.
1993	Peter MacDonald, once chairman of the Navajo Nation, is sentenced to prison for his role in a riot and for mismanaging tribal money. Roberta Blackgoat, a Navajo woman, is named one of "America's Unsung Women" by the National Women's History Project for her leadership in the environmental and civil rights movements.
1995	The Navajo Nation Council pardons Peter MacDonald.
1996	The Navajo win a lawsuit against a coal-mining company. The Navajo claimed that mining had damaged the environment.
2000	President Bill Clinton visits the Navajo Nation and announces a plan for cheaper phone service for the Navajo.

Glossary

chapter—a division of local Navajo government

clan—a related group of Navajo families

code talker—one of the Navajo soldiers who spoke in a secret Navajo code during World War II

conquistador—a Spanish word meaning "conqueror." A Spanish explorer who came to the Americas to claim land for Spain.

cradleboard—padded boards made to support a baby

Dine—a word meaning "the People" in Navajo. The Navajo name for themselves.

Enemyway—a religious ceremony used to cleanse the Navajo of foreign influences

fry bread—wheat dough fried in oil, a popular Navajo dish

hogan—a traditional Navajo house, usually eight-sided or round

Holy People—Navajo gods

irrigate—to water crops

mesa—a flat-topped hill

mutton—the meat of sheep

Nightway—a nine-day Navajo ceremony

pollen—the seed of the corn plant, sacred to the Navajo

radiation—dangerous, invisible rays given off by some substances

reservation—land set aside for Indian use

sand painting—religious designs drawn with sand. Also called dry painting.

singer—a Navajo religious leader

squash blossom—a style of Navajo jewelry

turquoise—a valuable blue-green stone

uranium—a radioactive mineral used in atomic weapons

way—a Navajo ceremony

The Way—a set of traditions that explains how the Navajo should live. Also called The Navajo Way.

To Find Out More

Books

Bial, Raymond. *The Navajo*. Tarrytown, NY: Marshall Cavendish, 1998.

Durrett, Deanne. *Unsung Heroes of World War II: The Story of the Navajo Code Talkers*. New York: Facts on File, 1998.

Grisham, Esther, Mira Bartok-Baratta, and Mira Bartok. *The Navajo*. New York: Harper Collins, 1996.

Roessel, Monty. *Kinaalda: A Navajo Girl Grows Up*. Minneapolis: Lerner Publications Company, 1993.

Roessel, Monty. *Songs From the Loom: A Navajo Girl Learns to Weave*. Minneapolis: Lerner Publications Company, 1995.

Organizations and Online Sites

Dine College (formerly Navajo Community College)
http://www.ncc.cc.nm.us/acad-body.html
This online site provides information about the first college established by an American Indian tribe.

Heard Museum
2301 North Central Avenue
Phoenix, AZ 85004
http://www.heard.org
Learn more about the Navajo and their neighbors at this museum that focuses on the American Indians of the Southwest.

Navajo Nation
http://www.navajo.org.
The best source for information about the government, current events, and traditions of the tribe.

The Navajo Times
http://www.thenavajotimes.com
The online site for *The Navajo Times*, the newspaper of the Navajo Nation, with current and past articles.

A Note on Sources

I was first introduced to Navajo culture by the mystery novels of Tony Hillerman. I was fascinated by the adventures of his Navajo detectives, Jim Chee and Joe Leaphorn, who combine Navajo traditions and modern police technique to solve crimes. To research this book, I made many trips to the Museum of the American Indian, located in New York City near my home. I began to read *The Navajo Times* on the Internet, and I read all the material on the home page of the Navajo Nation.

I found many articles in Arizona and New Mexico newspapers and read many books about the Southwest and the Navajo. One of the most helpful was *The Book of the Navajos* by Raymond Friday Locke. I quoted from this book on pages 5, 29, 32, 35, and 41 (bottom). I loved reading *Navajo Folk Tales* by Franc Johnson Newcomb. I learned much from an account by T. D. Allen, *Navajos Have Five Fingers*, in which the authors tell of running a health clinic in Navajo territory. *Woman of the Desert* by Gladys A. Reichard and *The Navajo* by Clyde Kluckhorn and Dorothea Leighton are two other classic books about the tribe that I enjoyed. I quoted from *The Navajo* on page 27. *We Are Still Here* by Peter Iverson gave me much information about the Navajo in the twentieth century. I quoted from this book on pages 37 and 41 (top). Other helpful books were *The Enduring Navajo* by Laura Gilpin, which I quoted on page 15, and *Lords of the Earth* by Jules Loh, which I quoted on page 16.

—*Geraldine Woods*

Index

Numbers in *italics* indicate illustrations.

About the Author

Geraldine Woods is the author of over forty books, most for young people. She teaches English to middle-school and high-school students in a New York City private school. She also directs the school's independent-study program. Every year she guides twenty students in independent-research projects, teaching them how to research a wide variety of subjects. She is married and the mother of one son, now a lawyer. She has always been interested in the culture and history of American Indians. One of the books she wrote for Franklin Watts, *Science of the Early Americas*, is an account of the scientific knowledge of ancient American Indians in both North and South America.